Hot Cars

CORVETTE

Lee Stacy

Rourke
Publishing LLC
Vero Beach, Florida 32964

D1164859

www.rourkepublishing.com

2004013020

LIBRARY OF CONGRESS CATALOGING-IN-PUBLICATION DATA
Stacy, Lee, 1961-
Corvette / Lee Stacy.
    p. cm. -- (Hot cars)
Includes bibliographical references and index.
ISBN 1-59515-209-1 (hardcover)
1. Corvette automotile I. Title. II. Series.

TL215.C6S73 2004
629.222'1--dc22
                            2004013020

For The Brown Reference Group plc

Managing Editor: Tim Cooke
Design Manager: Lynne Ross
Children's Publisher: Anne O'Daly
Production Director: Alastair Gourlay
Editorial Director: Lindsey Lowe

Picture Credits:
IMP AB

Printed in the USA

Some words are shown in **bold**, like this. You
can find out what they mean by looking at the
bottom right of most right-hand pages. You
can also find most of the words in the Glossary
on page 30.

Contents

Introduction 4

Corvette Sting Ray 6

BP Racer 10

1969 Corvette 14

1982 Corvette Collector Edition 18

1996 Corvette Grand Sport 22

1998 Corvette 26

Glossary 30
Further Information 31
Index 32

Introduction

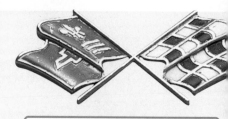

The name *corvette* originally meant a small, fast warship. In 1953 General Motors (GM), the world's biggest automobile manufacturer, introduced a new sports car to its Chevrolet division. The new car was fast but small—there was only room for a driver and one passenger. GM named the new car the Corvette.

By the 1960s the Corvette, also known as the Vette, had caught the country's imagination.

The Corvette emblem is based on two flags. One is a winning checkered flag. The other is red with the Chevrolet symbol and a fleur-de-lis. This represents the French roots of the company's founder, Louis Chevrolet.

In 1969 General Motors made the first of the third-generation Corvettes. More powerful than earlier Vettes, it could go from 0 to 60 mph (97 km/h) in 5.5 seconds.

It became known as the nation's favorite sports car. The Vette has remained extremely popular. There have been five generations of Vettes. Each had new models that were improvements on the ones before. Some of the most important Vettes include the Sting Ray, BP Racer, the 1969 model, the Collector Edition, the Grand Sport, and the first of the fifth generation, the 1998 model.

In 1998 General Motors produced the first models of the fifth generation of the Vette. Critics say that the new generation is one of the best.

Only a few Grand Sports were made in 1996 to mark the end of the fourth-generation Vette. It was painted to look like the 1960s classic, the BP Racer.

Corvette Sting Ray

When Corvette built the first Sting Ray in 1963, America finally had a sports car that could perform better than European models. The car's lightweight fiberglass coupe body was based on a racing car designed in 1956. Its rumbling V8 engine and rapid acceleration soon made it a favorite among car fans. Models built since the 1960s may be quicker and handle better, but the Sting Ray is firmly established as "America's favorite sports car."

Vital Statistics for the Sting Ray

Top speed:	*135 mph (217 km/h)*
0–60 mph:	*5.6 seconds*
Engine:	*V8*
Engine size:	*427 ci (6,997 cc)*
Power:	*435 bhp at 6,200 rpm*
Weight:	*3,150 lb. (1,430.1 kg)*
Fuel economy:	*10.8 mpg*

*The **cockpit** is not luxurious, but it is functional. It gives the car the feeling of a hot rod.*

Milestones

1955
Zora Arkus Duntov becomes head of General Motor's Corvette program. He was the father of the Sting Ray.

1957
The Vette is the fastest production car in the world.

1963
The first Sting Ray production car is built.

1967
The Sting Ray L88 reaches the peak of performance with a V8 engine. The original body style changes.

... this Vette ... will leave most modern sports cars in a cloud of dust ... that snap-your-head back lunge of power still makes the Sting Ray America's favorite sports car.

The most popular Sting Ray for collectors is the 1963 coupe. It has a split rear window, but Chevrolet dropped the design because it spoiled rear vision. The split rear window reappeared in some later models to try to raise their value.

Cockpit   Area inside the car where the driver sits and operates the car.

Specifications

The Sting Ray's engine is set back in the car's frame. Having the engine there means that the overall weight of the car is distributed evenly. Modern users find the steering a little heavy, but for a 1960s car, the Sting Ray handled very well.

No trunk lid

There is no trunk lid. Access to the baggage area is from behind the car seats.

Optional side exhausts

Side exhausts are mainly chosen for their look. They are covered with a shield that has many slots in it. The shield prevents the driver or passenger from burning themselves.

 The Sting Ray was the first Corvette to have independent front and rear suspension.

 The Sting Ray started with Chevrolet's famous small-block V8 engine. In 1965 this was replaced by the new Mark IV big-block engine. The engine was enlarged again in 1966 and 1967 to 427 cubic inches (6,997 cc).

Fiberglass body

The Sting Ray body is made of fiberglass panels mounted on a traditional frame.

Alloy gearbox and clutch housing

The use of **alloy** in the gearbox and clutch housing made the car lighter and improved weight distribution.

Triple side vents

The arrangement of side **vents** changed over the years. This arrangement was available in 1965 and 1966.

Flip-up headlights

The headlights are raised and lowered by two special motors.

Alloy	A strong but lightweight metal made by mixing other metals
Vents	Openings that allow exhaust fumes to escape.

BP Racer

In 1963 General Motors introduced the first BP Racer. It was a similar shape to the Corvette Sting Ray. In other ways, the BP Racer was very different from a **street car**. It had a cut-down windshield, an overhead roll bar, and a metallic blue with white stripe paint finish. The BP Racer was Corvette's race car. It did well in races during the mid-1960s, but production of the model ended in 1967. Today it is one of the most prized American cars ever built.

Vital Statistics for the 1965 BP Racer

Top speed:	148 mph (238.2 km/h)
0–60 mph:	5.4 seconds
Engine:	V8
Engine size:	327 ci (5,359 cc)
Power:	375 bhp at 6,000 rpm
Weight:	3,150 lb. (1,429 kg)
Fuel economy:	12 mpg

Milestones

1963

General Motors introduces a new race car based on the popular Corvette Sting Ray.

1966

Racing driver Roger Penske steers the BP Racer to victory in a 12-hour endurance race.

1967

General Motors decides to end production of the BP Racer. The same year the car performs well at the international Le Mans race in France. It also wins the GT class at the Sebring endurance event.

The driver's seat in the BP Racer has a racer's belt attached. The five-point racer's belt gives the driver better protection if the car crashes at high speed.

Although a cut-down windshield and roll bar give the feeling of a pure-bred competition car, this Sting Ray is more civilized than many racers.

All Corvette BP Racers are collectors' items. The 1963 model is perhaps the most sought after. It was highly successful on the racing circuit. The Sports Car Club of America has sponsored races and exhibitions since the 1960s. The 1963 BP Racer has been one of the top performers in these races.

Street car   A car designed for driving on normal roads.

Specifications

General Motors adapted all the right things on the Sting Ray to make the BP Racer. The small but powerful V8 engine, the improved disc brakes, and better roadholding are a few of the changes that helped make the Racer a champion car in the GT class.

Twin-cam engines

The engine is a small-block V8, but at 327 cubic inches (5,359 cc) it can produce 375 bhp. In the 1960s it was the most powerful small-block engine made by Chevrolet.

Disc brakes

*The BP Racer has **disc brakes** on all four wheels. The disc brakes were designed to shorten stopping distance. They were also made to last longer than other disc brakes at the time.*

The engine is set far back in the BP Racer to try to balance the weight. It nearly works. The rear is slightly heavier than the front. This causes minor steering problems.

The BP Racer has a solid chassis, a specially designed suspension system, and a powerful V8 engine. These features make the car sturdy but responsive.

Exposed grill

Unlike the Sting Ray, the BP Racer does not have a large front fender. This means that the grill is exposed. The grill lets air circulate around the engine. This helps keep the engine from overheating.

Adapted cover storage

The area behind the seats was changed to make room for securing the roll bar. In the other Sting Ray models the area, known as the tonneau, was used to store the convertible top.

Fiberglass body

The body of all Corvettes is made out of **fiberglass.** This makes the cars lightweight, strong, and free from rust.

Disc brakes   A type of brake with a rotating disc inside the wheel mechanism. The wheel is stopped by a device that pinches the disc.

Fiberglass   A light but strong material made from glass in the form of fibers. It can be molded to nearly any shape.

1969 Corvette

General Motors, the parent company of Chevrolet Corvette, introduced the third-generation Corvette in 1969. The new range was not popular. It was criticized for being too big and brash, especially when compared to European sports cars. Even Corvette's critics had to admire the power of the engine, however. The model's basic engine was 427 cubic inches (6,997 cc), enough to send the car racing at speeds up to 135 mph (217.3 km/h).

Vital Statistics for the 1969 Corvette

Top speed:	*135 mph (217.3 km/h)*
0–60 mph:	*5.5 seconds*
Engine:	*V8*
Engine size:	*427 ci (6,997 cc)*
Power:	*435 bhp at 5,600 rpm*
Weight:	*3,145 lb. (1,427 kg)*
Fuel economy:	*10 mpg*

The instrument panel in the 1969 Corvette has large, easy-to-see gauges.

Milestones

1966

The body design of the 1966 Corvette is based on the shape of a shark.

1968

The 1968 model is given high marks for performance by professional test-drivers.

1969

General Motors introduces several changes to the design of the Corvette, both inside and out. Among the changes are new *taillights* and reshaped doors. Several different-sized engines are available for the Corvette.

Though most of the Chevrolet Corvette's weight is over the front wheels, it can hold a line or corner with most any other sports car.

Most 1969 Corvettes had a V8 engine with a maximum power of around 435 bhp. A few, such as this L88, had a larger engine. The L88 could reach 500 bhp. Today it is considered a collectors' item.

Taillights   Warning-indicator lights positioned at the rear of the car.

Specifications

Most people thought that the Sting Ray was a better-looking car than the third-generation Corvettes. However, even most Sting Ray fans were impressed by the large Chevrolet V8 engine in the 1969 Corvette.

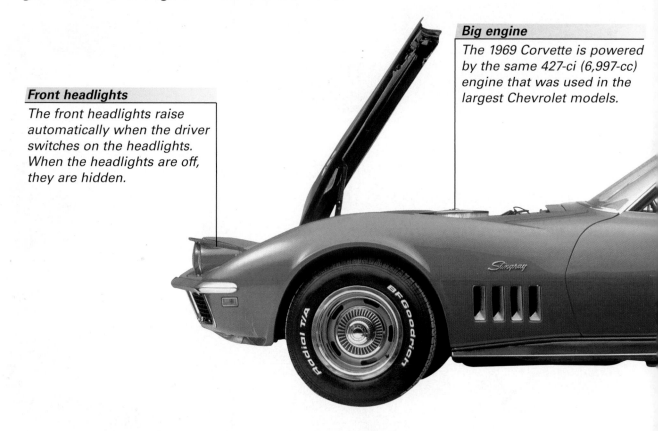

Big engine

The 1969 Corvette is powered by the same 427-ci (6,997-cc) engine that was used in the largest Chevrolet models.

Front headlights

The front headlights raise automatically when the driver switches on the headlights. When the headlights are off, they are hidden.

The 1969 Corvette was available with five different-sized engines. The smallest choice of engine was 427 cubic inches (6,997 cc). The largest was the powerful L88.

One of the criticisms of previous Corvettes was that the cockpit was too cramped. To correct this, the 1969 model was given a smaller steering wheel, among other changes.

Optional wheel control

To control wheel spin during hard acceleration, General Motors made a limited-slip **differential** for the 1969 Corvette. The device cost thousands of dollars extra.

Hard top available

An optional hard top can be attached to the convertible for added protection.

New interior

The 1969 Corvette had a smaller steering wheel and thinner door panels to make the cockpit roomier.

Differential A mechanism that makes the wheels on either side of an axle spin at either the same rate or, for instance, when turning a corner, at different rates to maintain the car's overall balance and speed.

1982 Corvette Collector Edition

In 1982 General Motors stopped making the third-generation Corvette. The model needed updating. For example, it used the Sting Ray's **chassis**. To mark the end of the third generation, General Motors made a special version of the Vette, called the Collector Edition (CE). Today the model is highly prized by collectors.

Vital Statistics for the 1982 Corvette Collector Edition	
Top speed:	125 mph (201.2 km/h)
0–60 mph:	8.0 seconds
Engine:	V8
Engine size:	350 ci (5,735 cc)
Power:	200 bhp at 4,200 rpm
Weight:	3,425 lb. (1,554 kg)
Fuel economy:	20 mpg

The interior of the 1982 Corvette was far more comfortable than earlier models.

Milestones

1976

More than 45,000 Corvettes have been built. The design of the body is still based on earlier models.

1978

To celebrate the Corvette's 25th anniversary, the car is given a new rear window.

1980

By rebuilding the body with more aluminum, GM makes the Corvette 250 lb. lighter.

1982

General Motors makes some 25,000 of the new Corvettes.

Best of all, the handling and steering are truly in the sports car league, reminding you that, despite its luxury content, it is still … America's Sports Car.

Only limited numbers of the 1982 Corvette were made. That makes it one of the sports cars most valued by collectors. The model had special wheels and a silver-and-beige paint finish.

Chassis   The supporting frame of the car on which the body is fixed.

Specifications

The 1982 Corvette is referred to as the Collector Edition. This is because General Motors decided to make only a few thousand to mark the end of the third-generation Corvette. The model has many special features lacking on earlier Corvettes.

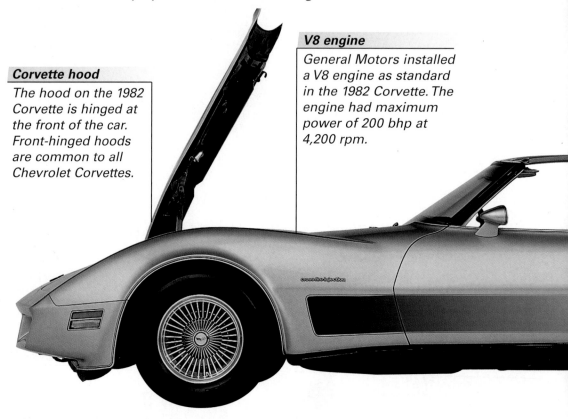

Corvette hood

The hood on the 1982 Corvette is hinged at the front of the car. Front-hinged hoods are common to all Chevrolet Corvettes.

V8 engine

General Motors installed a V8 engine as standard in the 1982 Corvette. The engine had maximum power of 200 bhp at 4,200 rpm.

The T-top glass roof panels in the 1982 Corvette are etched in bronze. The panels can be removed and stored in the area behind the seats.

One of the many special features of the limited-edition 1982 Corvette are the aluminum wheels. They look similar to the propellers of a jet engine.

More aerodynamic

Few major changes were made to the 1982 Corvette except that the front and rear ends were slightly reshaped. The new shape made the model more **aerodynamic** than other third-generation Corvettes.

Lift-up rear window

The lift-up rear window in the 1982 Corvette is mounted on twin hydraulic arms. When raised, it gives easy access to the rear of the car.

Special interior

The 1982 Corvette has silver-colored upholstery and door trim. These were special additions because only a few thousand cars were made.

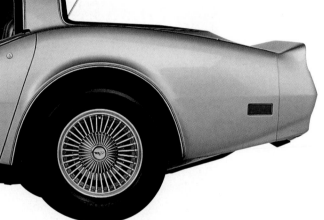

Aerodynamic	Designed to pass smoothly through the air.

1996 Corvette Grand Sport

The 1996 Grand Sport was designed to be the last of the fourth-generation Corvettes. Chevrolet created the car to celebrate the end of the series. It was made to look similar to the classic BP Racer of the early 1960s. The Grand Sport has a wide white racing stripe that runs the length of the top of the vehicle.

Milestones

Vital Statistics for the 1996 Corvette Grand Sport

Top speed:	168 mph (270.4 km/h)
0–60 mph:	4.7 seconds
Engine:	V8
Engine size:	350 ci (5,735 cc)
Power:	330 bhp at 5,800 rpm
Weight:	3,298 lb. (1,496 kg)
Fuel economy:	21 mpg

1984

The first fourth-generation Corvette is introduced. A 5.7 liter engine, called the L83, powers the new model. The chassis is stiff and the outside sleek, giving the fourth-generation Corvette the look and feel of a race car.

1990

The ZR-1, a 32-valve alloy engine designed by Lotus, becomes available in limited numbers in the Vette.

1996

The Grand Sport ends the fourth-generation Vette.

The interior of the Grand Sport is leather. The Grand Sport symbol is embroidered into the backrest of each seat.

Its stable road manners and flat-out handling leave the driver with a strong feeling of confidence and enthusiasm. It's a driving enthusiast's dream come true.

Some Grand Sports included added extras that helped the car turn corners tighter at high speed. These extras included a thicker anti-roll bar, firmer **shocks**, and stiffer springs.

Shocks Short for "shock absorbers," which are attached to the suspension system and help the car ride smoothly.

Specifications

It is not just the race-car paint finish that makes the Grand Sport a modern classic. Underneath the hood is a V8 engine, the LT4. It was designed to give the last of the fourth-generation Corvettes 10 percent more power than the previous engine.

LT4 engine

*Called the LT4, the new V8 engine in the 1996 Corvette is 340 ci (5,735 cc). It has modified **pistons** and cylinder heads, which yield 330 bhp.*

Six-speed manual

The transmission of the Grand Sport is only available as a six-speed manual. General Motors decided that an automatic transmission could not handle the increased power of the LT4 engine.

The Grand Sport had improved power steering and race-car suspension. In 1996 test drivers singled out these features for special praise.

Around a thousand LT4 Grand Sports were made. Although only a few years old, the model is already considered by many to be a collectors' item.

Large rear tires

The wide, high-performance tires on the 1996 Grand Sport are made especially for the model by Goodyear. The rear tires are larger than the front ones.

Paint finish

The 1996 Grand Sport has a paint finish based on an earlier Corvette, the BP Racer of the 1960s. The body is colored metallic blue. A white racing stripe runs the length of the car. There are red hash marks on the front of the car on the driver's side only.

Rear window

The wide glass rear window can be raised. This had been a standard feature on Corvettes since the early 1980s.

Piston	A small movable rod fitted into an engine's cylinder shaft and attached at its base to a crankshaft. The up-and-down movement of the piston draws gasoline into the engine and rotates the crankshaft.

1998 Corvette

Many people thought that the 1998 Corvette was a "return to greatness." General Motors had introduced the fifth generation of Corvettes a year earlier. One of the major differences between the 1997 and 1998 models was that the latter included a convertible. The fifth-generation Corvette is comfortable and stylish and takes the model to a higher level. It holds its own against competitors, such as the Ferrari F355 and the Lotus Esprit V8.

Milestones

1990

With a powerful V8 engine, the Corvette can accelerate from 0 to 60 mph (97 km/h) in under five seconds.

1997

General Motors introduces a new generation of Corvette but without the V8 engine. The 1997 version has the L51 engine. Other differences include a longer *wheelbase* than previous models.

1998

The convertible is introduced. It is not as aerodynamic as the coupe, but it is still fast.

Vital Statistics for the 1998 Corvette

Top speed:	175 mph (281.6 km/h)
0–60 mph:	4.7 seconds
Engine:	V8
Engine size:	347 ci (5,686 cc)
Power:	345 bhp at 5,400 rpm
Weight:	3,220 lb. (1,461 kg)
Fuel economy:	20.2 mpg

The cockpit in the sophisticated 1998 Corvette combines comfort with easy-to-use controls.

The L51 V8 engine revs instantly in response to its new electronic throttle control and sends the car soaring to 60 mph in less than five seconds ...

The 1998 Corvette is the fifth generation of the model. Wider and taller than the previous models, the 1998 Corvette stands out as one of the most stylish ever made. It is also the fastest Corvette to date. It can reach speeds up to 175 mph (281.6 km/h).

Wheelbase   The distance between the front and back axles.

Specifications

The 1998 Corvette is considered by many experts to be one of the best sports cars in the world. When designing the model, General Motors placed performance on an equal footing with luxury. The 1998 Corvette is a joy to drive in every way.

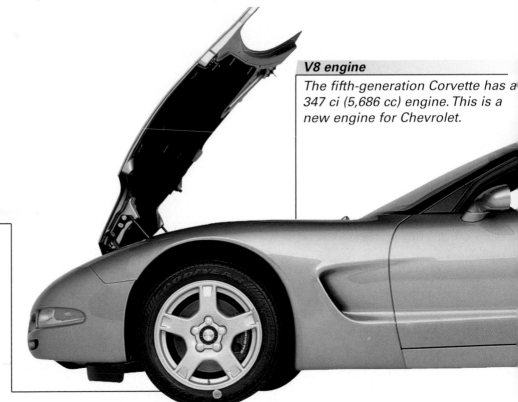

V8 engine

The fifth-generation Corvette has a 347 ci (5,686 cc) engine. This is a new engine for Chevrolet.

Tire-pressure monitor

The fifth-generation Corvette has a tire-pressure monitor that warns the driver when the tire pressure is low.

The basic 1998 Corvette comes with a four-speed automatic **transmission**. A six-speed manual transmission is available at extra cost.

The body of the 1998 Corvette is made of fiberglass. This is not new. There is a long tradition of Corvettes having a fiberglass body on a steel chassis.

Automatic traction control

*If a wheel begins to slip, an automatic wheelspin controller switches on. It reduces the power or speed until the **traction** is under control.*

Foldaway roof

The roof foldaway is under a body-colored cover behind the car seats.

Rear six-speed transmission

The transmission in the 1998 Corvette is located in the rear of the car. This gives more even distribution of the car's weight.

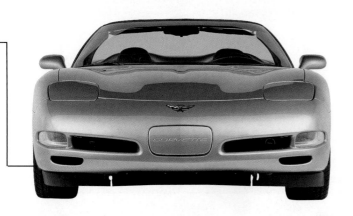

Traction	How well the wheels grip or stay in contact with the road surface when the car is moving.
Transmission	The speed-changing gears that transmit power from the engine to the axle.

Glossary

aerodynamic (ARI o dy NAM ik): *Designed to pass smoothly through the air.*

alloy (AL OY): *A strong but lightweight metal made by mixing other metals.*

chassis (CHASS ee): *The supporting frame of the car on which the body is fixed.*

differential (DIF uh REN shul): *A mechanism that makes the wheels on either side of an axle spin at the same rate or, when turning a corner, at different rates to maintain the car's overall balance and speed.*

disc brakes (DISK BRAYKS): *A type of* brake with a rotating disc inside the wheel mechanism. A clip pinches the discs to stop the wheels.

fiberglass (FY bur GLAS): *A light but strong material made from glass in the form of fibers. It can be molded to nearly any shape.*

piston (PIS tun): *A rod fitted into a cylinder shaft and attached at its base to a crankshaft. The up-and-down movement draws gasoline into the engine and rotates the crankshaft.*

shocks (SHOX): *Short for "shock*

absorbers," devices that smooth out a bumpy ride.

street car (STREET KAR): *A car designed for driving on normal roads.*

traction (TRAK shun): *The grip between a tire and the surface of the road.*

transmission (trans MISH un): *Speed-changing gears that transmit power from the engine to the axle.*

wheelbase (WE ul BASE): *The distance between the front and back axles.*

Further Information

websites

www.chevrolet.com/corvette
Chevrolet Corvette

www.corvettemagazine.com
Corvette Magazine.com

http://auto.howstuffworks.com/engine.htm
How Stuff Works: Car Engines

www.corvettemuseum.com
National Corvette Museum

books

● Beck, Paul. **Uncover a Race Car: An Uncover It Book.** Silver Dolphin Books, 2003.

● Egan, Peter. **This Old Corvette: The Ultimate Tribute to America's Sports Car.** Voyageur Press, 2003.

● Falconer, Tom. **The Complete Corvette: A Model-By-Model History of the American Sports Car.** Crestline Publishing, 2003.

● Montgomery, Andrew. **Corvette: The Definitive Guide to the All-American Sports Car.** Thunder Bay Press, 2003.

Index

A
aerodynamic 20, 21, 26
alloy 8, 9, 22
automatic wheelspin controller 28
axle 17, 27, 29

B
BP Racer 5, 10–13, 22, 25

C
chassis 12, 18, 19, 22, 28
Chevrolet 4, 7, 8, 12, 14–16, 20, 22, 28
Chevrolet, Louis 4
clutch 8
cockpit 6, 7, 16, 17, 26
Collector Edition (1982) 5, 18–21
coupe 6, 7, 26
crankshaft 25
cylinder heads 24

D
differential 16, 17
disc brakes 12, 13
Duntov, Zora Arkus 6

E
emblem 4
engine 13, 14, 16, 22, 25, 27, 29

F
fender 12
Ferrari F355 26

G
fiberglass 6, 9, 13, 28
5.7 liter engine 22
gauges 14
gearbox 8
General Motors 4, 5, 10, 12, 14, 16, 18, 20, 23, 26, 28
Goodyear tires 24
Grand Sport 5, 22–25

H
headlights 9, 16
hood, front-hinged 20

L
L88 6, 14, 16
Le Mans (race) 10
Lotus Esprit V8 26
LT4 engine 24

M
Mark IV engine 8

N
1998 Corvette 5, 26–29
1969 Corvette 4, 5, 14–17

P
Penske, Roger 10
piston 24, 25

R
racer's belt 10
racing car 6
racing stripe 22, 25
rear window 7, 18, 21, 25

S
roadholding 12
Sebring (race) 10
shark 14
shock absorbers 23
side exhausts 8
Sports Car Club of America 11
steering wheel 16, 17
Sting Ray 5–13, 16, 18
street car 10, 11
suspension 8, 12, 23, 24

T
taillights 14, 15
tonneau 13
transmission 24, 28, 29
twin-cam engine 12

U
upholstery 21

V
V8 engine 6, 8, 12, 15, 20, 26, 28
vents 9

W
wheelbase 26, 27